COPYEDITING WITH AN ATTITUDE

How To Proof And Edit Ads
And Other Marketing Copy

written by Freddy Tran Nager
Founder & Creative Strategist, Atomic Tango LLC
Adjunct Professor, University of Southern California

illustrated by Mark Armstrong

ATOMIC TANGO

An Atomic Tango Production
Made In L.A.

Copyediting With An Attitude:
How To Proof And Edit Ads And Other Marketing Copy

written by Freddy Tran Nager
illustrated by Mark Armstrong
cover design by Anthony Wiktor

First Edition

ISBN-13: 978-0-692-14483-1

Atomic Tango LLC
11301 Olympic Boulevard #445
Los Angeles, California 90064
www.AtomicTango.com

CONTENTS

PREFACE: ENOUGH ALREADY (AND I'M TALKING TO MYSELF)

Nobody's perfect. Certainly not me. After decades of writing and editing professionally, I still create typos in my emails, articles, and comments to students. (Oh, the irony and embarrassment of writing "please proofread you're work.")

In fact, I bet you'll find at least one typo hiding in this book.

So I regularly have to tell myself to review my writing. Again. And again. And again.

But eliminating errors isn't enough. We copywriters must also be efficient and effective. In short: less waste, more impact.

Copyediting With An Attitude will help you eliminate errors and enhance your writing. Following its recommendations might even get you hired or promoted. (If combined with expert schmoozing, of course.)

That said, this book isn't just for copywriters. It can help anyone who works with words or wordsmiths:

1. Creative directors and other execs who hire and manage copywriters.
2. Journalists, bloggers, or creative writers.
3. Publication editors.
4. Students and professors who need to rescue their prose from the cursed "academic voice."
5. Anyone who just wants to have more fun writing.

Note that this book doesn't cover all the rules of grammar. Not even close. That's because we copywriters regularly violate the rules. Like writing in sentence fragments. And starting sentences with conjunctions. And generally striving to "Think Different" (as Steve Jobs said differently).

That doesn't mean you should ignore the rules. To position yourself as a creative rebel and not a grammar school dropout, you need to follow them most of the time.

If you do need grammatical guidance, read *The Elements Of Style* by William Strunk, Jr. & E.B. White. (All writers should have a copy of Strunk & White chained to their desks.)

One final note: The initial letters of my copyediting criteria — Flawless, Active, Concrete, Tight — together spell "F.A.C.T." That acronym doesn't mean anything; I just love playing with words. And if you hope to succeed as a writer, you should love wordplay, too.

And that includes copyediting with an attitude.

Freddy Tran Nager
Los Angeles
December 2018

INTRO: PUT THE PRO IN PROOFREAD

Before diving into copyediting, try to make all the following practices hard habits to break.

1. Proofread, wait 24 hours, then proofread again.

Creative copy miraculously changes the day after you write it. What seemed brilliant and witty yesterday will sound contrived and cheesy today.

Reason one: If you love writing, you'll get deeply involved in your work. Although emotions fuel creativity, they also warp perception — especially if you mix them with late hours and strong drinks. By the next day, your feelings will have tempered, so your words won't emote the same vibes.

Reason two: Working on a computer will tire you out, and weary writers don't notice details. Humans weren't meant to stare into a light for hours on end — that's usually an end-of-life experience.

Of course, putting off proofreading for 24 hours means you need to complete your draft in advance, especially if your client or boss adores revisions. While procrastinating is as common among creative people as wearing black, pad your schedule to allow thorough proofreading. (Plus, Murphy's Law guarantees that your printer, computer, or internet service will crash the day your assignment is due.)

2. Proofread out loud.

Since your ears can detect problems your eyes might miss, proofread out loud, preferably in a private place where people won't throw things at you. (Note: whispering should suffice.)

Proofreading out loud will help you detect whether your work sounds conversational or convoluted. Most marketing copy should have a style your audience will understand and enjoy. By contrast, consider this exercise in awkwardness:

"Our variety of products is undoubtedly largely where we get our popularity from."

Does it make sense? Yes. Is it free of typos and misspellings? Yes. Is it good to go? Not even close. Your eyes might notice that; your ears definitely will.

In addition, some sentences look fine on paper, but when you read them out loud, you'll run out of breath. That tells you they need trimming or breaking up. (More on that in Act 5.)

Bonus Tip: Learn writing by osmosis.

I regularly read, listen to, and analyze the work of top novelists, screenwriters, and comedians. Some of their talent rubs off on me... or so I like to think.

To enhance your writing, read the work of talented people out loud. You might notice that simply hearing their style will gradually enhance your vocabulary and timing.

This doesn't mean copy them, since plagiarism is a cardinal sin that will doom you to an eternity of reading nothing but academic journal articles.

Reading great writing can also help you break out of ruts and blocks — particularly if you just spent what felt like an eternity reading nothing but academic journal articles.

3. Bribe a friend or family member to proofread.

What sounds clever to you might not make sense to others. What seems like a harmless joke might offend everyone else.

That's because we writers create backstories in our minds — stories we don't put on paper. We visualize certain readers who already know our subject. We imagine specific actors playing the roles. And if we listen to music while writing, we think our copy possesses its rhythm and hues, which our readers won't detect.

We need someone else's perspective.

So recruit a literate friend who does not work with your client, product, or campaign. Your coworkers have insider knowledge, so they might miss gaps in your writing.

For example, while developing ads for Toyota, my teammates and I knew what "ABS" meant, but few consumers know that ABS stands for "antilock braking system." Instead, they might wonder, "This car has stomach muscles?"

Now all that proofreading might sound like a lot of work — and it is. But that extra effort will justify the big bucks you charge for copywriting. It will also keep your client from replacing you with her nephew, the English major.

Yes, brilliant ideas matter, but details do, ~~to~~ too.

ACT 1: MAKE IT FLAWLESS

Eliminate all errors. Mistakes make you look replaceable by your client's nephew, the English major.

Ads containing errors will also make your clients look untrustworthy. Their potential customers might think, if this company can't handle advertising, how can I trust them with my taxes, my surgery, my lawsuit, my education, or my burrito?

So, first and foremost, copyediting must catch and correct all errors. Sounds obvious — do you need a book to tell you that?

Some people apparently do.

I recently received an email from a book-writing service that stated, "We are offering you this once is a lifetime chance..." Catch that? The email went on to promise "perfection in your publication," but that one glitch exposed their true aptitude.

(By the way, we marketers should never promise "perfection," since that provokes critical thinkers into scrutinizing everything we do with a vengeance.)

To make your copy flawless, follow these steps...

1. Use Microsoft Office spelling and grammar check.

This also sounds obvious, yet I receive many Word documents containing highlighted errors — the most unforgivable kind.

Of course, you shouldn't rely on computerized proofreaders alone. They can't check names or numbers, and they'll overlook near misses ("fiend" instead of "friend").

Bonus Tip: Compose everything in Word.

When writing emails, blogposts, or social media posts, compose in Word, which has better proofreading tools than those other platforms. Doing so also protects your work should your web browser crash. (Been there, cursed that.)

2. Look for commonly confused terms.

The Internet tortures grammar nerds with flagrant misuses of "your/you're," "there/their/they're," "whose/who's," and the frequently missed "its/it's." Word's grammar check catches most of those mishaps, but if you want to write professionally, you must learn the difference between homonymic pronouns.

Other mistakes will likely slip past Word's artificially intelligent proofreaders, sometimes to comedic effect:

- **"bated breath" vs. "baited breath":** The former means holding your breath in great suspense; the latter means you have a fish hook with a worm in your mouth.

- **"honored" vs. "humbled":** The former means you're flattered; the latter means you're brought down to earth, even humiliated. I often hear award recipients claim they're "humbled," which means the experience shamed them. You can "humbly accept an honor," meaning you're doing so modestly, but saying you're "humbled" by it insults the award giver.

- **"literally" vs. "figuratively":** The former means your words are factual and straightforward; the latter means metaphorical. So if you say, "This book literally blew my mind," you're describing a messy scene that requires a hazmat cleanup.

- **"peak" vs. "pique":** The former means to bring something to its highest point; the latter means to stimulate. So if you say, "This book peaked my interest," you're claiming it fascinated you more than anything ever in your life. (To which I respond, "Thanks, I'm ~~humbled~~ honored.") The appropriate term: "piqued my interest."

- **"complimentary" vs. "complementary":** The former means flattering or free (as in complimentary WiFi); the latter means different things fitting so well they enhance each other, as in a copywriter complementing a designer.

- **"loose" vs. "lose":** The former means uncontained or not tight; the latter means to suffer defeat. The statement, "They will loose the game," doesn't make sense, but I understand the mix-up. (The pronunciation of "lose" also makes no sense.) Just remember this: "The moose and goose are on the loose." Any other use means you lose.

3. Verify spellings of names and proper nouns.

Never misspell a client's name or brand, even in a text message. That's a remarkably easy way to get fired. This step includes checking capitalization, since many brands (particularly dotcoms) have capital letters mid-name, such as YouTube. Quick: how would you capitalize the following?

facebook
firefox
in-n-out burger
instagram
microsoft
netflix
snapchat
spacex
starbucks
starkist
wordpress

4. Triple check contact info.

Review phone numbers, email addresses, URLs, and street addresses. Have someone else check, too. A typo in a phone number could lead to a stranger getting harassed, which could provoke a lawsuit. And as the gods of the internet would have it, every mistyped web address leads to a porn site.

5. Evaluate consistency.

Did you notice that every numbered subhead in this book starts with a verb, ends with a period, and uses sentence case for capitalization? If you're like most readers, you didn't, but exacting bosses and clients might. All items in a list or series should share the same format (all nouns, all calls to action, etc.).

More importantly, stay consistent with tense (past, present, future) and voice (first, second, third). Whatever you choose is fine; just stick with it. I've read corporate content that starts in third person ("The gas company values its customers...") before sliding into first/second ("We would like you to know..."). Having multiple personalities works for actors, not brands.

To help maintain consistency, work with your client to create a style guide that addresses writing choices like these:

- **Pronouns**. How should you refer to their company ("it," "they," or "we") and audience ("you," "they," or "our customers")?

- **People.** When you repeatedly refer to someone, should you use their first name or last after the first mention? And do you use titles (Mr., Ms., Dr., Prof., etc.)?

- **Punctuation.** Can you use contractions, such as "can't" or "don't"? How about "ain't"? How should you punctuate acronyms and abbreviations, e.g., "USA" or "U.S.A.", "Ph.D." or "PhD"? And should you use the Oxford comma, which sets off the last item in a series, e.g., "I love my favorite foods, books, and cats"? (Drop the comma after "books" to see why I endorse using it.)

Bonus Tip: Create a brand bible.

While setting style guidelines, establish branding rules like these:

- **Naming.** What abbreviations and nicknames can you use for the company and its products? For example, the University of Southern California may officially be "USC" and informally "SC," but never "Southern Cal" or "SoCal." In automotive marketing, some brands eschew articles: it's "Camry" not "the Camry." (I always thought that sounded weird, but those are Toyota's rules.)

- **Slang and profanity.** Can you use current terms ("OMG," "sick," "lit") or dated ones ("cool," "fab," "rad")? How about four-letter words, including thinly veiled expletives ("WTF," "f*ck") and friendlier variations ("crap," "kick ass," "damn")?

- **Competitive urges.** Can you ever talk about competitors? If so, in what way?

6. Eliminate needless repetition.

This one's tricky and a bit subjective.

You should eliminate word repetition that looks and sounds awkward, such as, "Athletes everywhere drink our drink."

Also look for awkward repetition in consecutive sentences: "When you're working out, you need to drink lots of fluids, or you'll get dehydrated. So you should be drinking at least two bottles of water during your workout to avoid dehydration." That passage not only repeats variations of "work out," "drink," and "dehydration," but also "you."

So buy yourself a good thesaurus and learn synonyms.

That said, strategic word repetition can sound catchy, almost poetic. Consider FDR's "The only thing we have to fear is fear itself." And sometimes repetition abets wordplay: "StarKist doesn't want tuna with good taste, they want tuna that tastes good." Just make sure your deliberate, strategic repetition doesn't come across as laziness.

Likewise, avoid repeating the same structure in consecutive sentences, otherwise your copy will sound unnatural at best, or bad poetry at worst. Example:

"If you need a cat, you've come to the right place. With our massive selection, you'll find the cat you want. Once you find the cat you want, you can adopt it without hassle. After you adopt the cat, you'll get the friendliest service."

Notice the structure? Subordinate clause + clause, subordinate clause + clause, *ad nauseam*. In addition, the sentences run roughly the same length. No normal person would speak like that, yet many writers perpetrate this crime. Instead, employ a variety of structures: short, long, complex, simple.

"Looking for a cat? You've come to the right place. Our massive selection means you'll find the one you want. You can adopt it without hassle, and our post-adoption service is the friendliest. Meow!"

That said, structure repetition can sound catchy, too: "You're bored. You're lonely. Here's a cat. You're welcome."

So how do you know whether to choose repetition or variety? Ask two questions:

1. **What's the purpose of the copy?** For a radio spot that needs to attract attention and be memorable, enjoy your poetic license. For a corporate white paper that needs to convey facts to a serious audience, stick to straight prose.

2. **How does it sound?** Yes, proofread out loud.

You'll find exercises at the end of this book to practice your copyediting skills. In the meantime, here's a check list for all kinds of writing, from tomes to tweets.

PROOFREADING CHECK LIST

Initial and date each item when complete:

1. Used Microsoft Office spelling and grammar check ____

2. Looked for commonly confused terms _____

3. Verified spellings of names and proper nouns _____

4. Triple checked contact info _____

5. Evaluated consistency _____

6. Eliminated needless repetition _____

ACT 2: MAKE IT ACTIVE

Over 50 years ago, ad legend David Ogilvy laid down the law: "You cannot bore people into buying." Yet how often do you encounter a modern brochure, website, or commercial that puts you to sleep faster than a Monday morning status meeting?

To avoid inducing comas in your audience, remember this: If you get bored writing something, imagine how it will make your readers feel.

I can't make you love writing, but I will show you how to make it active. And I don't mean use exclamation marks or ALL CAPITAL LETTERS, unless you're creating a comic book or monster truck ad. Few people like shouters.

Instead, use strong words and structures, and start by replacing the weakest of verbs...

1. Replace "be" verbs (including "am," "is," "are," "was," "were," etc.).

Use a yellow highlighter to mark all the "be" verbs in your copy. If it now resembles a mini lemon grove, you need to juice it up with stronger verbs.

While you can't replace all variations of "be" — sometimes they defy substitution, and sometimes they work best — do make the easy fixes. You'll often find a stronger verb hiding in plain sight: for example, change "our burgers are tasty" to "our burgers taste great." Additional examples:

- change "that dress is hot" to "that dress looks illegal" or "that dress turns heads dangerously fast"

- change "be alert for cats" to "stay alert for cats"

- change "our website is located at www..." to "visit our website at www... "

Note how the last sentence changes from a bland statement to a call to action. Additional conversions:

- change the "will be doing" structure to simply "will do" (e.g., "the cats will be playing all night" to "the cats will play all night")

- change the "am going to" structure to simply "will" (e.g., "I am going to feed the cats later" to "I will feed the cats later") except when "am going to" refers to travel ("I'm going out")

- change the "am able to" structure to simply "can" (e.g. "Are you able to herd cats?" to "Can you herd cats?")

You'll find another common "be" offense clogging up resumes, cover letters, and executive bios: "am responsible for." So instead of writing "I am responsible for leading creative teams," simply say "I lead creative teams." Additional examples:

- change "I am responsible for organizing" to "I organize"

- change "I am responsible for ad writing" to "I write ads"

- change "I am responsible for meeting planning" to "I plan meetings"

If you need to show executive-level responsibilities, use strong verbs like "manage," "supervise," or "direct," as in "I direct product branding." After all, "responsible for" doesn't mean you actually do anything. A child may "be responsible for" cleaning her room, even though she never does it.

2. Make passive voice active.

This fix usually requires little more than a basic subject-verb-object structure. For example, change "this ad should be proofread" to "proofread this ad."

Some writers use passive voice because they don't know who to designate: "This ad should be proofread... by you... or Bob ... or Jane... or whoever..." Leave ambiguity to politicians. In marketing, pick a subject. Additional examples:

- change "our cat food is recommended by 9 out of 10 veterinarians" to "9 out of 10 veterinarians recommend our cat food"

- change "your payment should be sent by April 15" to "send your payment by April 15"

- change "most of their decisions are made carefully" to "they make most of their decisions carefully"

In other passive-voice cases, you might need to alter the verbs. For example, change "the concert was performed last night" to "the concert happened last night" or "the concert rocked the arena last night." You'll notice that also eliminates "be."

3. Replace "there is" and "it is" at the beginning of sentences with a specific subject.

We tend to use "there is" and "it is" when speaking quickly or sounding pompous, such as "it is written..." But as sentence openers, "there is" and "it is" can sound vague and weak, and copywriters get paid to sound precise and enthusiastic.

For example, change "it is exciting to write" to "writing is exciting." That makes the action the subject. (Now inject more energy by replacing the "be" verb and saying "writing excites me.") Additional examples:

- change "there are many reasons to adopt cats" to "we have many reasons to adopt cats"

- change "there's a cat video on the home page" to "the home page features a cat video"

- change "it's going to be kitten season soon" to "kitten season is coming" (or "get ready for kitten season," which replaces the "be" verb and creates a call to action).

One more note...

You'll find classic uses of "be" in literature ("To be or not to be...") and advertising ("Be all that you can be..."). I love those examples, but their authors wouldn't have made a living had they used "be" everywhere else.

As mentioned, you can't eliminate all uses of "be" — I use it frequently — but give your marketing copy (and career) more life by leaning toward "not to be."

ACTIVE WRITING CHECK LIST

Initial and date each item when complete:

1. Highlighted all "be" verbs in copy _____

2. Replaced "be" verbs with active verbs _____

3. Replaced passive voice with active voice _____

4. Replaced "there is" and "it is" with stronger subjects _____

ACT 3: MAKE IT CONCRETE

You know what bores most readers?

Not simplicity. We like statements that, well, just do it.

Not serious subjects, either. A talented writer can make even complicated, technical topics entrancing. (Read *Wired* magazine for proof.)

To bore your readers, write in abstractions: passage after passage of vague concepts that ignore the senses. If you avoid taste, touch, smell, sound, or vision, your readers' minds will wander or fade to black. They might read the entire document but not retain a word.

Consider this "marketing" description (I changed the company name to protect the guilty):

"Initech transforms how teams build technology. Its customers accelerate the delivery of innovative products with proven solutions, which combine Initech's intelligent product strategy and roadmapping software with full-stack, agile development services. With decades of experience building disruptive technology in the heart of Silicon Valley, Initech's team shares a proven track record of enabling companies to achieve breakthrough results with software and services."

How much of that did you hack your way through? How much do you remember mere seconds after reading it? Aside from "heart of Silicon Valley," this copy contains as much actual heart as the center of a bagel.

You'll find product descriptions, brochures, and website "about us" pages stuffed with similar fluff. If a lawyer, professor, or engineer wrote them, that's understandable. (Not good, but we get it.) If a marketer wrote them, that's unforgivable.

So when someone tells you that "people don't like to read," ask them "what" and "why." Adolescents consume megaton tomes about Harry Potter. Sports fans devour articles filled with analysis. Political junkies inhale pages of beltway punditry.

People even like to read marketing. Really. Savvy consumers (the ones who influence others) read thousands of words on select products and services. They enjoy browsing enthusiast magazines, catalogs, and reviews, both online and off.

What people don't like to read is copy without substance. Here's how to fix it...

1. Avoid slang and jargon.

Slang doesn't make copy persuasive or interesting; it makes it flabby and dull. Claiming that your product is "cool" or "hip" or "chic" means that it's not. It also doesn't mean anything —what exactly does "chic" look, taste, feel, smell, or sound like?

For example, every year a major stationery retailer advertises "cool back-to-school supplies," a description that no student has uttered ever. In addition, pandering to teens or cultural segments with slang ("this joint is on fleek!") usually backfires by making the brand sound old and patronizing.

Likewise, in corporate America, jargon doesn't sound smart or professional; it sounds pretentious, as if the writer is overcompensating for a lack of talent or knowledge. While some professionals (surgeons, engineers, filmmakers) use jargon to quickly converse with colleagues, that doesn't apply to marketing. (For insights on how jargon is destroying civilization, read the book *Why Business People Speak Like Idiots: A Bullfighter's Guide*.)

To sound smarter, replace slang and jargon with active verbs and concrete nouns that readers can readily understand and remember. For example, don't use "solutions" to describe your work; get specific, such as "marketing plans" or "solar energy systems." Don't tell everyone you're "chic"; describe your style, such as "youthful looks from London in the Sixties."

Two other generic words to eliminate from your vocabulary: "thing" and "stuff." (Unfortunately, someone with a stunted vocabulary coined the vapid term "Internet of Things.")

Additional examples:

- leverage
- cutting edge (and, worse, bleeding edge)
- disruptive

- revolutionary
- hot
- cold
- hip

Replace those vapid words with vivid details.

Consider this proposed restaurant copy: "Our delectably delicious dishes will delight your palate." Despite the snappy alliteration, it's redundant and generic. Fortunately, the restaurant didn't use it — they fired the agency.

Rather, if a restaurant invests time and passion into their food, return the favor by describing their dishes in detail: "Dip your fork into our signature dessert, and you'll discover dark chocolate ganache spread between two moist layers of buttery pound cake, practically melting before your eyes..."

Yes, that means you'll have to use and know your client's products. (Tough job, right?)

2. Get even more specific.

By listing the ingredients, the revised dessert description stands out and sticks. Instead of "delectable dish," the reader remembers "chocolate" and "pound cake."

Already have concrete descriptions? Try to make them even more specific. For example, change "enjoy live music in our lobby" to "enjoy live Cuban jazz in our Havana-themed lobby." Additional examples:

- change "imagine driving this car on the open road" to "imagine cruising through the scenic twists of the Pacific Coast Highway"

- change "the festival features dancers" to "the festival features samba dancers in flowing dresses of gold"

- change "this computer will help you create" to "this laptop will help you write your dream novel"

3. Purge clichés.

You know them when you hear them: expressions so overused, misused, and abused, they no longer have meaning.

Exhibit A is "authentic," which used to mean "genuine," but which some people now use to describe anything they like (even though something can be authentically evil). Other meaningless clichés include "transparent," "we care," "quality," and "please hold — your call is important to us."

For fun, give clichés a twist. Start with something readers recognize, but change the ending. Examples:

- "If at first you don't succeed, hire a new agent."

- "Seeing is believing — unless your vision is fuzzy, so get your eyes checked today."

- "If looks could kill, you'd get arrested for wearing those shoes."

Bonus Tip: Write at the level of your audience.

As a young copywriter, I wanted to flaunt my college-enriched vocabulary. But this was the music industry, where my boss told me, "Most people here can barely read." And he was talking about other record executives.

Of course, he exaggerated. A little. Some of the world's most literate people are musicians. Yet most music fans don't want ads that sound like literary journal articles. Consequently, my boss made me replace any word that average teenagers wouldn't use.

Similarly, my entrepreneurial finance professor, the great James Stancill, taught us "The Rule of 16" for pitching investors: Use no more than 16 words in 16 seconds in a way a 16-year-old could understand. That works even though most investors are older, wealthier, and more educated than the general public.

To determine the level of your audience, simply speak with them. At the least, go online to read and watch what they enjoy, including their own writings and videos.

Then share your findings with your clients, who might think their customers care about "world-class, cutting-edge, disruptive solutions." Show what they really talk about.

CONCRETE WRITING CHECK LIST

Initial and date each item when complete:

1. Replaced all slang and jargon _____

2. Made nouns as specific as possible _____

3. Deleted all clichés or gave them a twist _____

ACT 4. MAKE IT TIGHT

"That's great — now cut it in half."

My boss in the music industry told me that daily — several times daily. No matter what I wrote, he made me cut it and cut it again and cut it once more. (And, yes, he would have made me cut that last sentence.)

I initially resented all that cutting. As the saying goes, writers hate killing their babies. But now I thank him. Long before Twitter's tight limits, he taught me to economize verbally. So today I cringe when I see writers fluff up copy ("gotta increase that page count!") or get lazy.

Marketing has no room for excess, particularly online, since reading text on screens causes eyestrain.

In addition, readers reward us with their time and attention, so don't waste it. That doesn't mean omit necessary info or persuasive copy — you still need to sell. "Tight" means replacing unnecessary words with more valuable ones.

I recommend two approaches to tightening...

1. Pretend that words cost money.

Some publications pay writers by the word — a mistake, since that incentivizes larding up copy. Now pretend you're an editor eliminating words so that you pay for only what you use. You still need compelling text — you can't have an empty or boring publication — but you must make it profitable.

For example, let's say each word costs you $1. "We are committed to achieving the highest possible levels of customer satisfaction" would cost you $12, while "We strive to completely satisfy our customers" would cost $7. (Plus, the shorter version kills the "be" verb.) Additional examples:

- change "we plan to be showcasing cats all through the evening" ($10) to "we'll showcase cats all night" ($5 — I'm a stingy editor who counts contractions as one word)

- change "our team is able to handle a majority of the challenges that come with cats" ($15) to "we can handle most cat challenges" ($6)

- change "we are going to conduct the research and perform the writing responsibilities on the topic of cats" ($17) to "we'll research and write about cats" ($6)

- change "remember the time when we were training the cats?" ($9) to "remember when we trained the cats?" ($6) or even "remember training the cats?" ($4)

- change "this is making me feel justified about wanting to rescue cats" ($12) to "this justifies rescuing cats" ($5)

- change "we made the switch to the new and improved cat litter" ($11) to "we switched to the new cat litter" ($7) (As other advertising critics have noted, something can't be *both* new and improved.)

Copyediting for conciseness takes practice. Even I still find excess words in my work. (For example, the first draft of that sentence read, "After decades of doing it, I still find words I can cut in work I completed.") And future editions of this book will probably be even tighter.

2. Break up chewy sentences.

While proofreading out loud, note whenever you stumble over words or pause for breath. Your sentence is likely "chewy" — more than a mouthful — and needs editing.

Take the following "death sentences" from the book *Strategic Business Forecasting* by Ronald Sugar & Simon Ramo:

"Having predicted the range, we then can examine the possible consequences to the future of our own particular activity at each limit with confidence that we probably have covered the situation, certainly not completely, or maybe not even adequately, but at least somewhat usefully. If either of the two limits were to occur and if we had earlier concluded that we could not survive with one, or worse, with either, then the forecasting process already will have been of some help to us in our management duties because we might have acted earlier to better the future as a result of our prediction attempts."

Forget a mouthful — that's like chewing a ball of tin foil. Try to read that whole thing in 1 or even 2 breaths.

You'll notice that chewy writing contains too many clauses and phrases. That paragraph's first sentence alone contains 5 prepositional phrases: "to the future" + "of our own" + "at each limit" + "with confidence" + "at least somewhat usefully."

Now use your highlighter to mark up your own writing. If a sentence contains more than 3 clauses or prepositional phrases, it likely needs chopping into bite-size pieces.

Bonus Tip: Say it with pictures.

I hear my designer friends gasping, "Freddy, the writing zealot, says replace words with images?!"

Yes — with qualifications.

As mentioned, I disagree with the notion that people don't like to read. In addition, words and descriptions help build brands and introduce new concepts and products. And when writing for websites, you must have text to feed search engines.

But sometimes showing beats telling.

For example, if you want to increase cat adoptions, you can write paragraphs filled with descriptions and statistics... or simply show a photo of a moon-eyed kitten. In a business presentation, a clear graph showing how cats reduce vermin infestations can be more persuasive than a dozen bullet points.

Writing still matters, but if you replace some passages with pictures, the remaining words will receive more attention and have greater impact.

TIGHT WRITING CHECK LIST

Initial and date each item when complete:

1. Deleted unnecessary words _____

2. Proofread out loud _____

3. Marked all clauses and prepositional phrases _____

4. Broke up chewy sentences _____

TEST TIME

Ready to test your copyediting skills? Some of the following challenges have "right" answers, others have multiple options.

For the suggested outcomes and explanations, see the "Answers" section of this book. (No cheating!)

1. Find the errors:

A. Novelist Tom Robins once wrote, "Its never too late to have a happy childhood."

B. For those who like to seen and not herd, we have the perfect shoes. The new Adiddas Haute Pink shoes make a statement — a quite one, that is, thanks to silent cotton souls.

C. By using InstaGram influencers, we manage to peak the interest of millions of milennials.

D. Instead of substantiating they're criticisms with research, facts, statistics, ect., our critics use only antidotal evidence.

E. In the forward of her autobiography, JFK Rowling describes where he got the inspiration for the Hairy Potter series that she wrote.

2. Change the "be" verbs:

A. We will be announcing the winners at the cat show.

B. Our prices are the lowest in town!

C. These new jeans are soft to the touch.

    D. This book is going to be different from all the others.

    E. Is this result what you thought you would get?

3. Change passive voice to active voice:

    A. The first movie was released in late 2017.

    B. His book is considered "a classic" by experts worldwide.

    C. Her cat was awarded the Pulitzer Prize.

    D. The results have been posted on our Facebook page.

    E. The game was decided in the fourth quarter, when the Bruins were outscored by the Trojans 21-0.

4. Change "there is" and "it is" to stronger openings:

    A. There is no way anyone can beat our prices!

    B. It's getting hotter in California every year.

    C. There are many opportunities in Los Angeles!

    D. There are 3 great reasons to adopt a cat now.

    E. It is almost time for the holidays.

5. Replace vague terms, slang, and jargon with specific, concrete words. You have infinite choices, so enjoy yourself!

    A. Together we're the best. Los Angeles.

    B. Your cat will look totally stunning in one of our outfits.

C. We leverage best practices to maximize your bottom line.

D. Get ready for an amazing time in Las Vegas.

E. Our revolutionary solutions will disrupt the industry.

6. Eliminate unnecessary words.

A. Now is the time to start thinking about retirement plans.

B. People of all types love to eat our pizzas.

C. Our software solution could possibly increase the growth of your sales.

D. The state of California successfully hit more than a few targets in terms of water conservation.

E. The majority of our wine shipments go to customers in China.

7. Now for the real test: the following passages require a little of everything.

A. Hear at Gargantuan Trucks we have dozens of awesome trucks for you to choose from. There are big trucks, small tracks, luxury trucks and friendly sales people that are ready to make you a very special deal on the truck you have you're heart set upon.

B. In a world with out rules, there is only one man who stands between good and evil. But now he is going to encounter the biggest challenge of his life: himself. When a mad scientist clones him he suddenly finds himself fighting himself. Who is going to win? Audiences are waiting with baited breath to find out! Find out this summer when "Gargantuan Man" will be playing at a theater near you.

C. Do you ever ask yourself why you pay full retail pricing for stationary when you could save so much more money if you were to pay wholesale pricing? Its why the Gargantuan Office Supplies was established by us, it's founders in the year 1998 to save you money.

D. As a junior in highschool, now is the time for you to start thinking about where you would like to go to college in the future. We would like to suggest that you consider applying to Gargantuan University where you are going to find our stylin' professors ready to educate you on a hella good assortment of hot subjects you will like. And the vast majority of our alumni go on to good jobs after graduation.

E. Committed to excellence, Gargantuan Consulting is a leading consulting firm which leverages cutting-edge technology and best practices, which we are using to meet mission-critical enterprise needs. Based in Sillicon Valley, Gargantuan Consulting is staffed by graduates of leading Universities, that are all dedicated to partnering with you.

F. Welcome to the Gargantuan Fashions web site! There are so many things you can do on this site. For example on this website you are able to try on are stylish assotment of fashionable clothes using our virtual 3D mirror that shows you how awesome your going to look in 3-D when you wear them.

G. It's football season!And the L.A. Gargantuan Cats are ready to play! And that is fun for the whole family! So if your an LA resident and ready to have a fun time, discount tickets for locals are going on sale now!

H. There are so many ways to use Gargantuan Crackers. They are used for dipping in dips. You are also able to use them on salads, soups and making horderves. People are also using them when baking. We think they are delicious.

I. It is not unusual to think that our times are hard. That is why so many American people are turning to the new TV show about our times. It is called "Our Times with Bob Gargantuan." It is hosted by Bob Gargantuan, who was recently awarded an Emmy for his hosting work. Please visit the "Our Times" FaceBook page to see air times for "Our Times With Bob Gargantuan."

J. Gargantuan Advertising is looking to higher a writer to write advertising copy. This is an entry level position but you should have a minimum total of 3 years of working experience to qualify. If you are interested in this once in a lifetime opportunity to join a cool company, and you are looking to score some cool benefits and cool colleagues, your resume and for writing samples should be submitted on our website before the end of day on June 31.

ANSWERS

You'll find my recommended edits and corrected versions beneath each example. Take a second to consider why I made those changes. Your versions may differ from mine, and that's fine as long as they adhere to the guidelines in this book.

1. Find the errors:

A. Novelist Tom Robins once wrote, "Its never too late to have a happy childhood."

Errors: "Robbins" should have two b's; "Its" needs an apostrophe

Corrected: Tom Robbins once wrote, "It's never too late to have a happy childhood."

B. For those who like to seen and not herd, we have the perfect shoes. The new Adiddas Haute Pink shoes make a statement — a quite one, that is, thanks to silent cotton souls.

Errors: missing "be" after "like to"; "herd" should be "heard"; "we have the perfect shoes" isn't necessary; "Adidas" is misspelled; repetitive "shoes"; "quite" should be "quiet"; "souls" should be "soles"

Corrected: For those who like to be seen and not heard, the new Adidas Haute Pink shoes make a statement — a quiet one, that is, thanks to silent cotton soles.

C. By using InstaGram influencers, we manage to peak the interest of millions of milennials.

Errors: "Instagram" is misspelled; "peak" should be

"pique"; "millennials" is misspelled

Corrected: We use Instagram influencers to pique the interest of millions of millennials.

D. Instead of substantiating they're criticisms with research, facts, statistics, ect., our critics use only antidotal evidence.

Errors: "they're" should be "their"; "ect." should be "etc."; "antidotal" should be "anecdotal"

Corrected: Instead of substantiating their criticisms with research, facts, statistics, etc., our critics use only anecdotal evidence.

E. In the forward of her autobiography, JFK Rowling describes where he got the inspiration for the Hairy Potter series that she wrote.

Errors: "forward" should be "foreword"; "JFK" should be "J.K."; "he" should be "she"; "Hairy" should be "Harry"; "where he got the inspiration for" is a bit chewy; "that she wrote" isn't necessary

Corrected: In the foreword of her autobiography, J.K. Rowling describes what inspired her Harry Potter series.

2. Change the "be" verbs:

A. We will be announcing the winners at the cat show.

Corrected: We'll announce the winners at the cat show.

B. Our prices are the lowest in town!

   Corrected: We have the lowest prices in town!

C. These new jeans are soft to the touch.

   Corrected: These new jeans feel soft.

D. This book is going to be different from all the others.

   Corrected: This book will differ from the others.

E. Is this result what you thought you would get?

   Corrected: Did you think you would get this result?

3. Change passive voice to active voice:

A. The first movie was released in late 2017.

   Corrected: The first movie premiered in late 2017.

B. His book is considered "a classic" by experts worldwide.

   Corrected: Experts worldwide consider his book "a classic."

C. Her cat was awarded the Pulitzer Prize.

   Corrected: Her cat won the Pulitzer Prize.

D. The results have been posted on our Facebook page.

   Corrected: We posted the results on our Facebook page.

   Alternative: The results appear on our Facebook page.

E. The game was decided in the fourth quarter, when the Bruins were outscored by the Trojans 21-0.

   Corrected: The Trojans decided the game in the fourth quarter, outscoring the Bruins 21-0.

4. Change "there is" and "it is" to stronger openings:

A. There is no way anyone can beat our prices!

   Corrected: No one can beat our prices!

B. It's getting hotter in California every year.

   Corrected: California gets hotter every year.

C. There are many opportunities in Los Angeles!

   Corrected: Los Angeles offers many opportunities.

   Alternative: You'll find many opportunities in Los Angeles.

D. There are 3 great reasons to adopt a cat now.

   Corrected: You now have 3 great reasons to adopt a cat.

E. It is almost time for the holidays.

   Corrected: The holidays are almost here.

   Alternative: Get ready for the holidays.

5. Replace vague terms, slang, and jargon with specific, concrete words. You have infinite choices, so enjoy yourself!

A. Together we're the best. Los Angeles.

Note: This was an actual motto for L.A. developed in 1995 by a committee. (No surprise.) Naturally, it didn't stick. I bet you can create a better one.

B. Your cat will look totally stunning in one of our outfits.

Note: The Eighties popularized "totally" in teen speak, but it adds no value. And "stunning" doesn't say anything. Your version should help readers visualize the outfit.

C. We leverage best practices to maximize your bottom line.

Note: Typical corporate bull. Your version should describe the practices while promising to increase profits, not a bottom line. (Anything maximized can't grow any larger, so this passage isn't a promise, it's a threat.)

D. Get ready for an amazing time in Las Vegas.

Note: Vegas would kick you out for using that slogan. While the official slogan, "What happens in Vegas stays in Vegas" isn't specific, audiences can visualize the innuendo.

E. Our revolutionary solutions will disrupt the industry.

Note: More corporate hype that screams for details.

6. Eliminate unnecessary words.

A. Now is the time to start thinking about retirement plans.

Corrected: Start planning for retirement.

B. People of all types love to eat our pizzas.

   Corrected: Everyone loves our pizzas. ("Eat" is obvious
   — what else would they do with them?)

C. Our software solution could possibly increase the growth
   of your sales.

   Corrected: Our software could increase your sales.

D. The state of California successfully hit more than a few
   targets in terms of water conservation.

   Corrected: California achieved multiple water
   conservation goals.

E. The majority of our wine shipments go to customers in
   China.

   Corrected: We ship most of our wine to China.

**7. Now for the real test: the following passages require a little
of everything.**

A. Hear at Gargantuan Trucks we have dozens of awesome
   trucks for you to choose from. There are big trucks, small
   tracks, luxury trucks and friendly sales people that are
   ready to make you a very special deal on the truck you
   have you're heart set upon.

   Errors: "hear" should be "here"; "tracks" should be
   "trucks"; "friendly sales people" does not fit the series;
   people are "who" not "that"; "you're heart" should be
   "your heart"; "upon" should be "on"

   Corrected: Gargantuan Trucks offers dozens of vehicles:

big, small, luxury, and more. Find one you love, and our friendly sales team will make you a deal.

B. In a world with out rules, there is only one man who stands between good and evil. But now he is going to encounter the biggest challenge of his life: himself. When a mad scientist clones him he suddenly finds himself fighting himself. Who is going to win? Audiences are waiting with baited breath to find out! Find out this summer when "Gargantuan Man" will be playing at a theater near you.

 Errors: "with out" should be "without"; "mad scientist" is a cliché; "baited" should be "bated" (that said, does it matter what the audience is doing?)

 Corrected: In a lawless world, one man stands between good and evil — but can he defeat his toughest opponent: himself? When a scientist clones Gargantuan Man, anything can happen. See it this summer in theaters.

C. Do you ever ask yourself why you pay full retail pricing for stationary when you could save so much more money if you were to pay wholesale pricing? Its why the Gargantuan Office Supplies was established by us, it's founders in the year 1998 to save you money.

 Errors: "stationary" should be "stationery"; "it's" should be "its"

 Corrected: Why pay full retail for stationery when you can buy wholesale? Shop at Gargantuan Office Supplies — saving customers millions of dollars since 1998.

D. As a junior in highschool, now is the time for you to start thinking about where you would like to go to college in the future. We would like to suggest that you consider applying to Gargantuan University where you are going to find our stylin' professors ready to educate you on a hella good assortment of hot subjects you will like. And the vast majority of our alumni go on to good jobs after graduation.

Errors: "highschool" should be "high school"; dangling participle (the subordinate clause "as a junior in high school" modifies the next word, which should be "you"); "alumni... after graduation" is redundant; and as you surely noticed, the slang is painful

Corrected: As a high school junior, you should start exploring colleges. We invite you to apply to Gargantuan University, where you'll find enthusiastic professors and enriching programs, from art to zoology. Most of our graduates have successful careers. Want to join them?

E. Committed to excellence, Gargantuan Consulting is a leading consulting firm which leverages cutting-edge technology and best practices, which we are using to meet mission-critical enterprise needs. Based in Sillicon Valley, Gargantuan Consulting is staffed by graduates of leading Universities, that are all dedicated to partnering with you.

Errors: jargon and cliché hell; "consulting" and "which" are repeated in the same sentence; the first use of "which" should be "that"; "Silicon" is misspelled; "Universities" shouldn't be capitalized; structure of both sentences is nearly identical

Corrected: Based in Silicon Valley, Gargantuan Consulting combines technology and strategy to help you overcome challenges and achieve business goals. Our highly educated team will work with you to protect data, streamline operations, and meet other critical needs.

F. Welcome to the Gargantuan Fashions web site! There are so many things you can do on this site. For example on this website you are able to try on are stylish assotment of fashionable clothes using our virtual 3D mirror that shows you how awesome your going to look in 3-D when you wear them.

Errors: welcoming people to websites is a cliché; "website" is spelled two different ways; "try on are" should be "try on our"; "stylish" and "fashionable" are redundant; "assortment" is misspelled; "3D" is spelled two different ways; "your" should be "you're"

Corrected: Here at Gargantuan Fashions, you can virtually try on our designer outfits using a 3D mirror. And that's just a start!

G. It's football season!And the L.A. Gargantuan Cats are ready to play! And that is fun for the whole family! So if your an LA resident and ready to have a fun time, discount tickets for locals are going on sale now!

Errors: too many exclamation points; space needed between "season!" and "And"; "your" should be "you're"; "fun" is repeated; "L.A." is spelled two ways

Corrected: The L.A. Gargantuan Cats kick off August 28 — and local fans get discounts! Reserve seats now for your entire family.

H. There are so many ways to use Gargantuan Crackers. They are used for dipping in dips. You are also able to use them on salads, soups and making horderves. People are also using them when baking. We think they are delicious.

Errors: multiple voices (first, second, and third); "hors d'oeuvres" is misspelled; "they are delicious" sounds like it's referring to the people

Corrected: Enjoy Gargantuan Crackers with soups, salads, dips, hors d'oeuvres, and more. You'll love the garlic and pepper flavor!

I. It is not unusual to think that our times are hard. That is why so many American people are turning to the new TV show about our times. It is called "Our Times with Bob Gargantuan." It is hosted by Bob Gargantuan, who was recently awarded an Emmy for his hosting work. Please visit the "Our Times" FaceBook page to see air times for "Our Times With Bob Gargantuan."

    Errors: repetition; "Facebook" is misspelled; "Our Times with Bob Gargantuan" is inconsistently capitalized

    Corrected: When life gets hard, Americans watch "Our Times with Bob Gargantuan." Meet the Emmy-winning host and find air times on our Facebook page.

J. Gargantuan Advertising is looking to higher a writer to write advertising copy. This is an entry level position but you should have a minimum total of 3 years of working experience to qualify. If you are interested in this once in a lifetime opportunity to join a cool company, and you are looking to score some cool benefits and cool colleagues, your resume and for writing samples should be submitted on our website before the end of day on June 31.

Errors: "higher" should be "hire"; "advertising" repeated in same sentence; variations of "write" repeated in same sentence; false use of "entry level"; meaningless and repetitive use of "cool"; inconsistent numbering (numerical and spelled out); "for writing samples" should be "4 writing samples"; June 31 doesn't exist

Corrected: Gargantuan Advertising seeks a copywriter with at least 3 years' experience. Join our award-winning creative team and receive benefits ranging from vision care to unlimited vacations. Submit your resume and 4 writing samples on our website before July 1.

So how'd you do?

If you missed errors or didn't make the examples active, concrete, or tight enough, don't sweat it. Copyediting like a pro requires practice.

But do practice.

Suggestion: offer to copyedit your friends' resumes and LinkedIn profiles, where you'll likely find jargon, "be" verbs, abstractions, and passive voice. Along the way, you'll sharpen your skills and help your friends look even sharper.

Then, when they become rich and powerful, make them hire you to create their ad campaigns. (Talk about attitude...)

PARTING SHOT

I hope you found *Copyediting With An Attitude* useful. If so, please recommend it to friends and colleagues and review it on Amazon. (Yes, I'm marketing here.)

I also welcome both your questions and suggestions. Please drop me a line at AtomicTango.com.

In addition, I plan to write more books on business and creativity, so let me know what you'd like to read.

And above all, write on!

SO WHO DID THIS?

Freddy Tran Nager, Author

For nearly 30 years, Freddy has created marketing, media, and other mischief for clients, magazines, and his own company.

It all started after he received his bachelor's degree in East Asian Studies & Sociology from Harvard (a surefire recipe for unemployment). Freddy used his one marketable skill, writing, to land an advertising gig at MCA Records, where he worked on campaigns for Tom Petty, BB King, Elton John, and Mary J. Blige, to name a few. In 1994 he became Editor of *AMP: MCA Records Online*, one of the web's first entertainment sites.

After five years in the music industry — long enough for a non-musician — Freddy joined Saatchi & Saatchi as the agency's Sr. Interactive Copywriter. He spent the next two years writing Toyota's award-winning website and other digital media.

Always craving creative challenges, Freddy moved on to craft concepts, content, and campaigns for such brands as Nissan/Infiniti, the National Lampoon, Lexus, Royal Caribbean, and the world's first infomercial zine, IZ.

When the first dotcom boom went bust, Freddy decided to enhance his business skills by getting an MBA — what he describes as "the two most boring years of my life."

In 2007 (or '007, as he likes to say), Freddy launched the agency Atomic Tango to consult startups. The firm has since evolved to produce various forms of media, including this book.

Freddy also works as an Adjunct Professor at the University of Southern California. This book began as a handout for his students, who inspire him daily (and that's no joke).

When not writing, teaching, or consulting, Freddy spends quality time with his wife and too many cats.

Mark Armstrong, Illustrator

A full-time illustrator since 1989, Mark creates images that get brand content seen and shared.

He specializes in illustrations, cartoons, infographics, animated GIFs, slideshows, stop-motion animation, and videos. These take various forms: editorial art, marketing and social media campaigns, promotional videos, web graphics, and more.

Mark has worked with a diverse array of major brands, including Coca-Cola, Chick-fil-A, Guardian Life, RBC Dain, and Discover Financial Services.

To see more of Mark's creations, please visit markarmstrongillustration.com.